THE PHOTO·LIBRARY
4

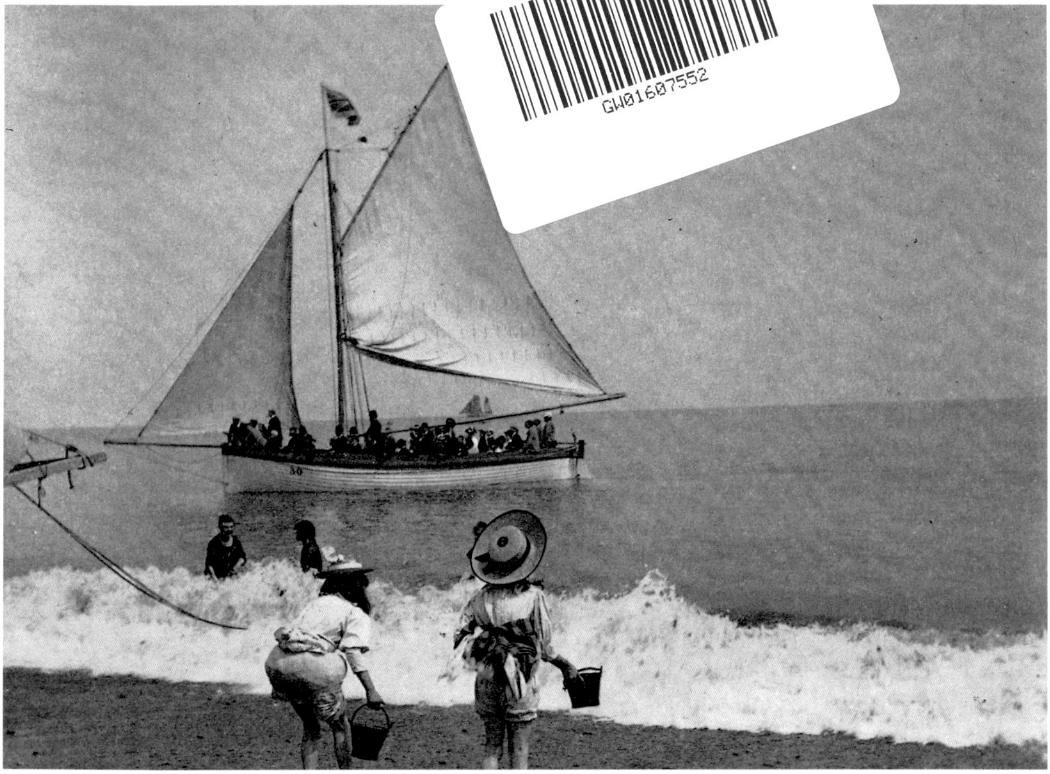

GW01607552

A Yarmouth Holiday

PHOTOGRAPHS BY PAUL MARTIN

Mark Haworth-Booth

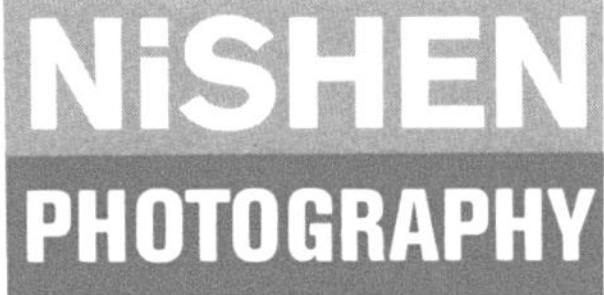

Paul Martin

A YARMOUTH HOLIDAY

Is this the most beautiful album of holiday photographs ever put together? The *Yarmouth Holiday* is like a collective holiday or a folk memory – a holiday our great- (or great-great-) grandparents might have enjoyed, or a holiday of our own – just out of the reach of memory (because we were too young) – or a holiday we might one day enjoy: one we can contemplate taking as we turn these pages.

Paul Martin was one of the first photographers to take snapshots of the kind we take today. The photographs in the album were his first efforts with a special new camera. It often happens that the possibilities of new technology in photography are investigated almost at once and completely – as, say, André Kertesz and Henri Cartier-Bresson were to test all the qualities of the Leica camera within a period of about five years (in the late 1920s and early 1930s). Paul Martin went off to Yarmouth, the popular holiday resort on the Norfolk coast, with a friend named Ted Smith and something called the 'Facile' Hand Camera, in the summer of 1892. Martin himself was then 28. He had just bought the camera.

The 'Facile' Hand Camera was a mahogany box camera which took a magazine of 12 glass plates. You could take a picture then turn a knob and another negative would drop into position (with a loud clunk, apparently). It was also a model of camera that could be used disguised as a parcel. Some early versions of it came wrapped in brown paper (impractical in normal European weather conditions). So the 'Facile' allowed quite quick exposures (in practice, one quarter to one tenth of a second), a measure of concealment if required – Martin had his camera disguised as a leather box – and the multiple shooting chances of a magazine. Furthermore, his camera – although bulky – did not need a tripod. All this offered exciting new opportunities. The previous generation of photographers had to prepare their negatives, one at a time, at the spot where the photograph was to be taken: they lacked concealment (no candid photography possible), spontaneity and experimentation from frame to frame, easy changing of camera height or angle. We take all of these features for granted. Paul Martin was one of the first to exploit the new possibilities and there is no mistaking the relish with which he did so.

He was actually born in France, as Paul Augustus Martin, at Herbeuville in 1864. His parents moved to Paris in 1869 and were among the unfortunate population which endured the Siege of Paris during the Franco-Prussian War in 1870. The Paris Commune followed – during which Martin senior barely escaped execution. The family settled in London the following year, where they found a home in Battersea, south-west London. At the age of 16 Martin was apprenticed as a wood engraver. He became a highly skilled engraver. His trade was to copy artists' sketches, and sometimes photographs, onto wood blocks for printing in the illustrated newspapers and magazines of the day. Of course, the skill he had so painstakingly learned was on its way out. Process engraving was to oust the old craft of wood engraving, and photographers would oust the old 'black and white' draughtsmen. However, Paul Martin had bought his first camera in 1884. He became a dedicated amateur. In 1888 *Amateur Photographer* magazine commenced publication, aimed precisely at isolated, ardent experimenters such as Paul Martin. He was also able to join

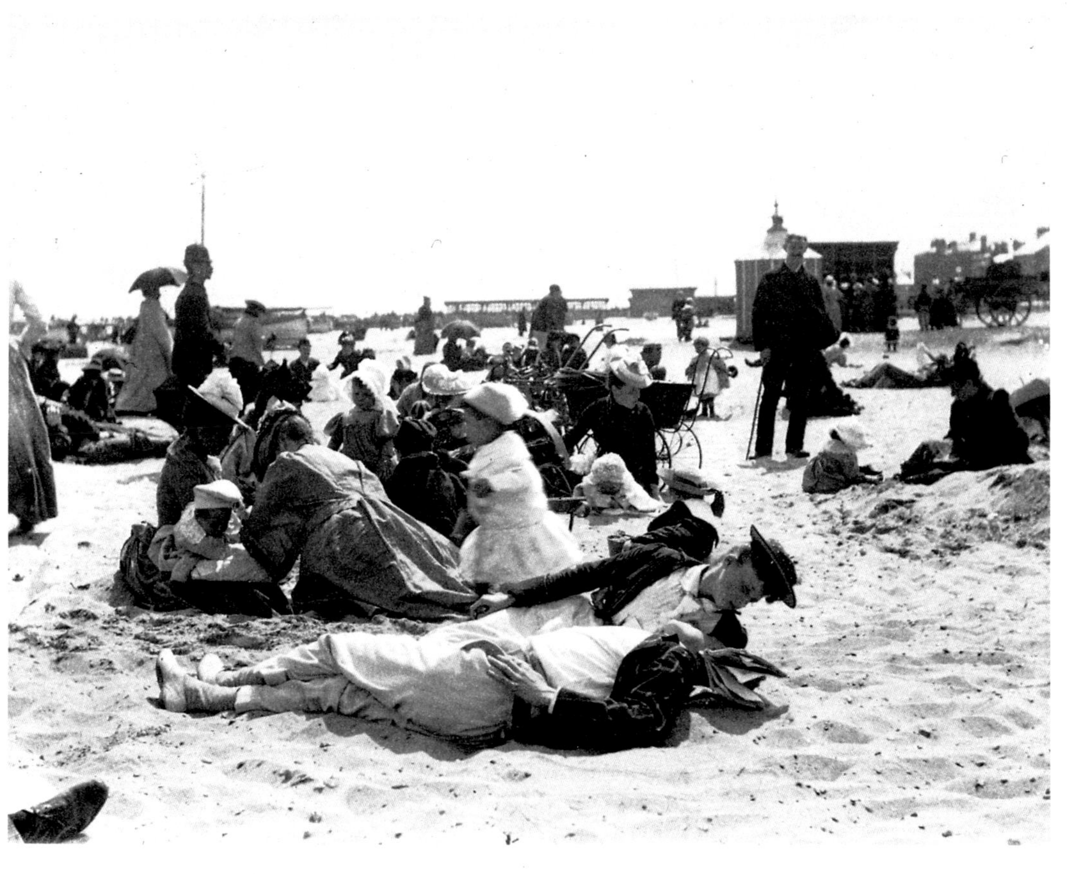

an active camera club (the West Surrey) and – at its exhibitions – to test his ambitions and results against lively and well-informed competitors. He began by exhibiting photographs taken in Battersea Park. His real talent became startlingly clear when he made his trip to Yarmouth on holiday in 1892.

As a wood engraver Martin was thoroughly used to interpreting complicated human events by means of an articulate schema of black and white and tones of grey. The seaside had already become a well-established subject for humorous illustrations in black and white. Dickens' illustrator John Leech made delightful drawings (translated into wood engravings), as did Richard Doyle, Randolph Caldecott and a host of others. The seaside was also an acknowledged site of comic literature and had been from the time of R. S. Surtees' *Jorrocks's Jaunts and Jollities* (1838). His sporting Cockney grocer, Mr Jorrocks, visits another resort, Margate in Kent, and finds it greatly to his liking. A guidebook of the 1840's remarks on the holiday-going of a 'host of merry mermaids, happy, no doubt, to exchange the dirty alleys of Whitechapel and the Minories (by Tower Hill), for a week's dip in the blue sea'. These seem to be the subject of most of Martin's Yarmouth photographs. He was clearly a jolly person and his photographs show that he enjoyed the uninhibited behaviour of his fellow-holidaymakers, fooling about on the beach, enduring that characteristic of an English holiday, the bracing east wind off the North Sea, striking heroic attitudes in cold sea water, and daring the waves to wet their bunched up summer skirts. Children cooperated with his camera, wittingly or unwittingly. It is likely that his friend Ted Smith, and perhaps others they befriended on holiday, appear in the album. Other pictures, however, do seem genuinely candid. He made pictures from an unusual, low viewpoint which gives his scenes an air of intimacy and also directness. The possibilities of the magazine of 12 negatives meant that he could expend half a dozen or more on capturing the cruise boat *Primrose* being launched. He noted himself that 'holidays were an expensive luxury – no work, no pay'. Maybe he took these photographs intending to exhibit them, sell prints and perhaps place them as illustrations for magazines. His hobby and relaxation was also a form of expression and a means of making money (and Martin went on to become a professional photographer seven years later).

Martin travelled out from Yarmouth to Wroxham Broad, where he photographed the Chinese lanterns, to Cromer – scene of his most compelling seaside photograph, of the girls caught by a wave, to Lowestoft and Gorleston, fishing ports near Yarmouth. Martin also photographed the working seamen of the place, the stock idealised by Dickens in the persons of Mr Peggotty and Adam in *David Copperfield.* However, it is his delicate, observant, humorous, experimental view of the Yarmouth Holiday which makes it so fresh and engaging today, like a holiday we think we might have had.

Mark Haworth-Booth

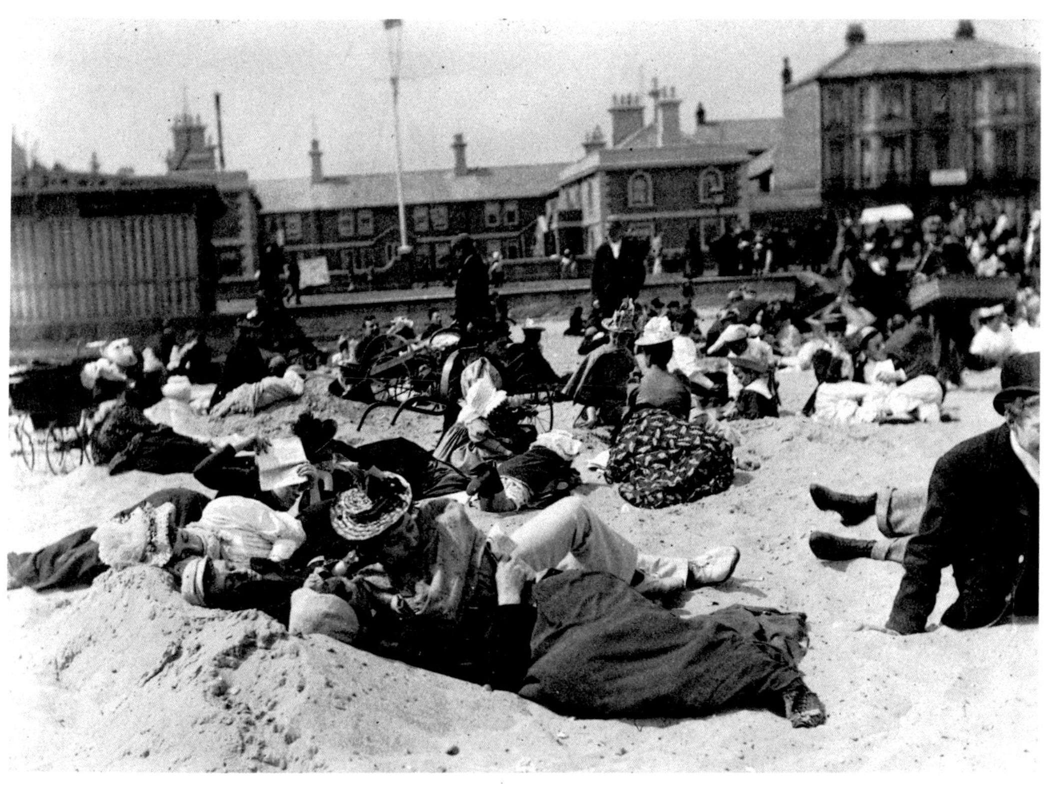

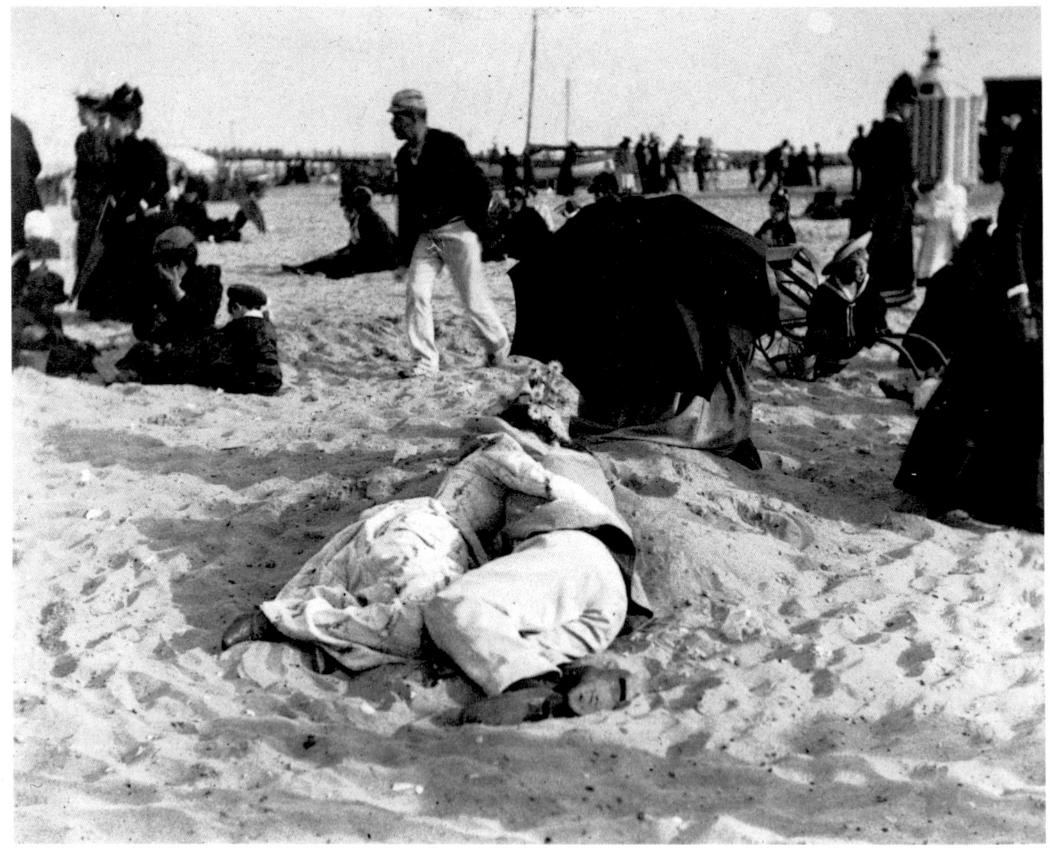

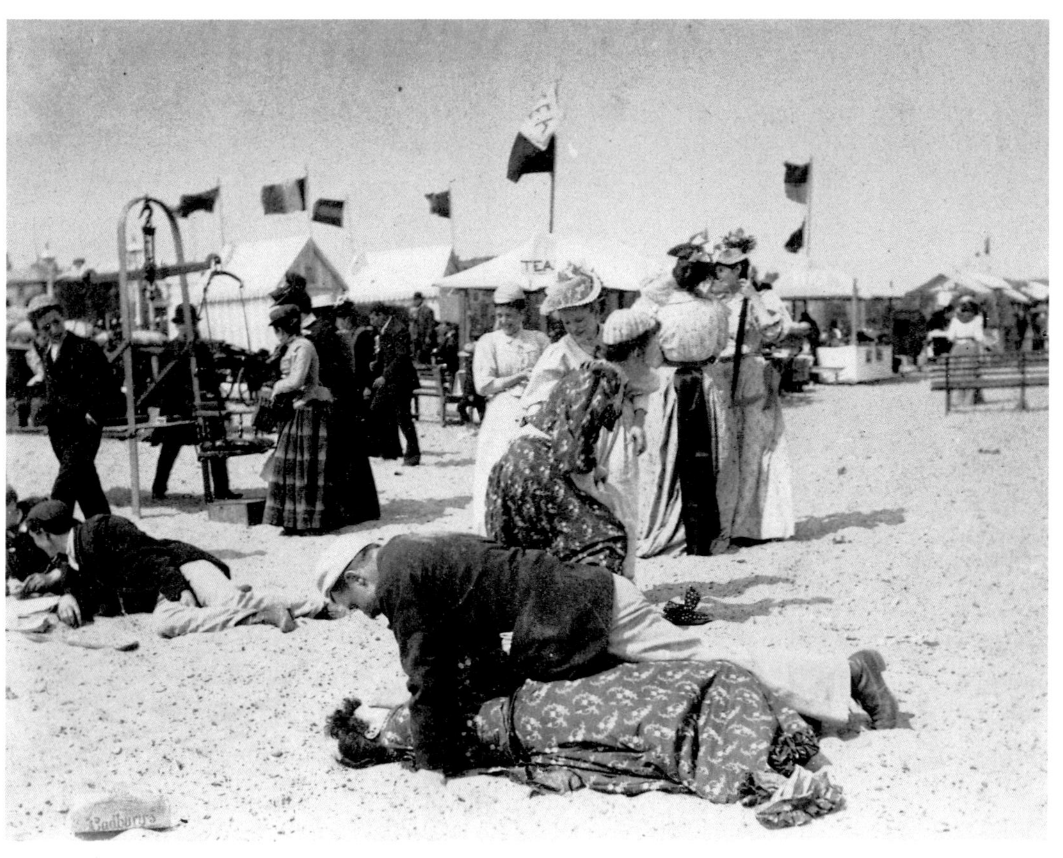
TEA

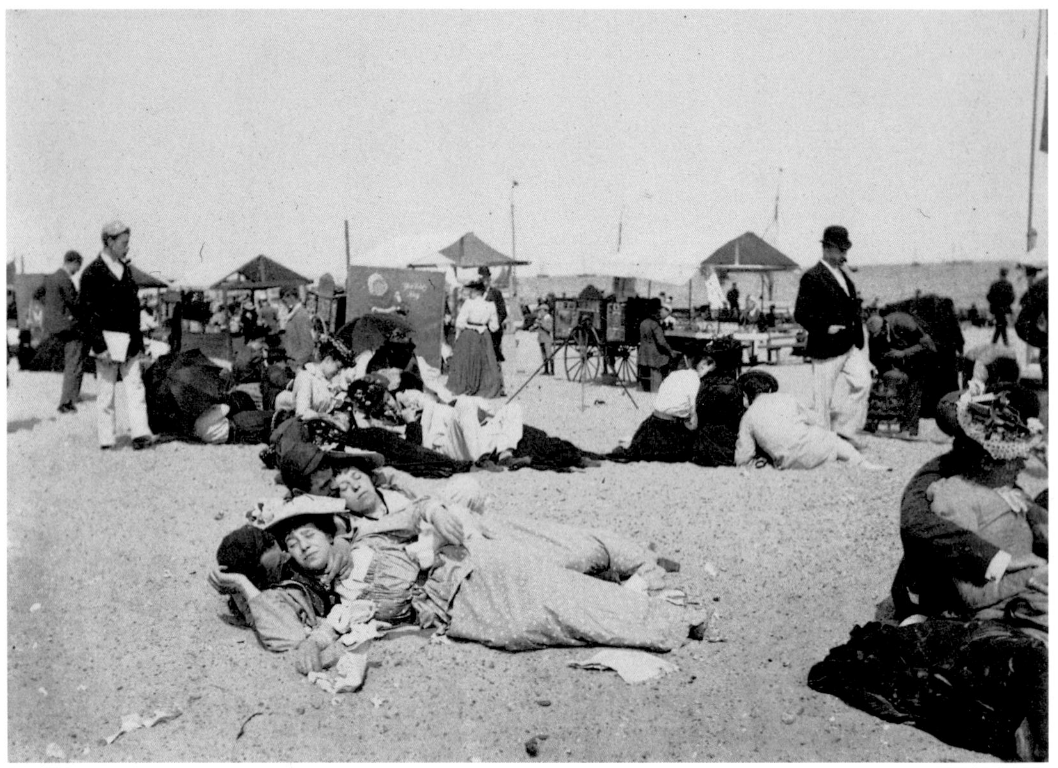

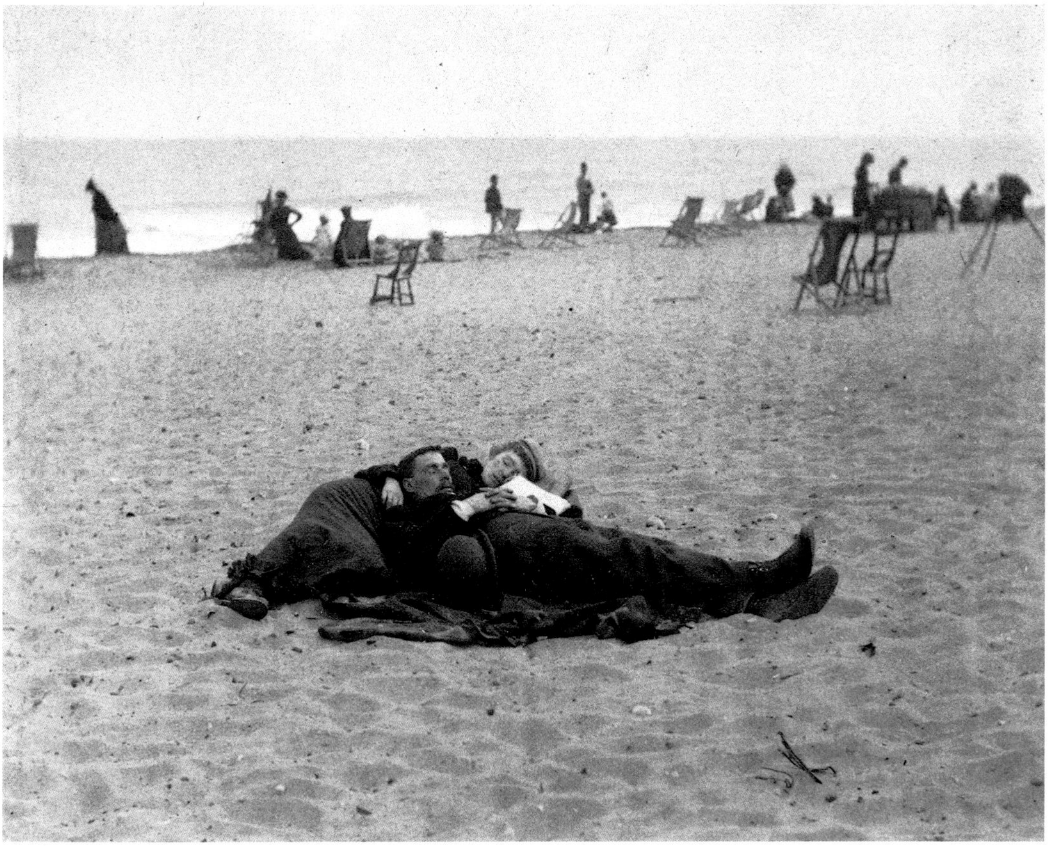

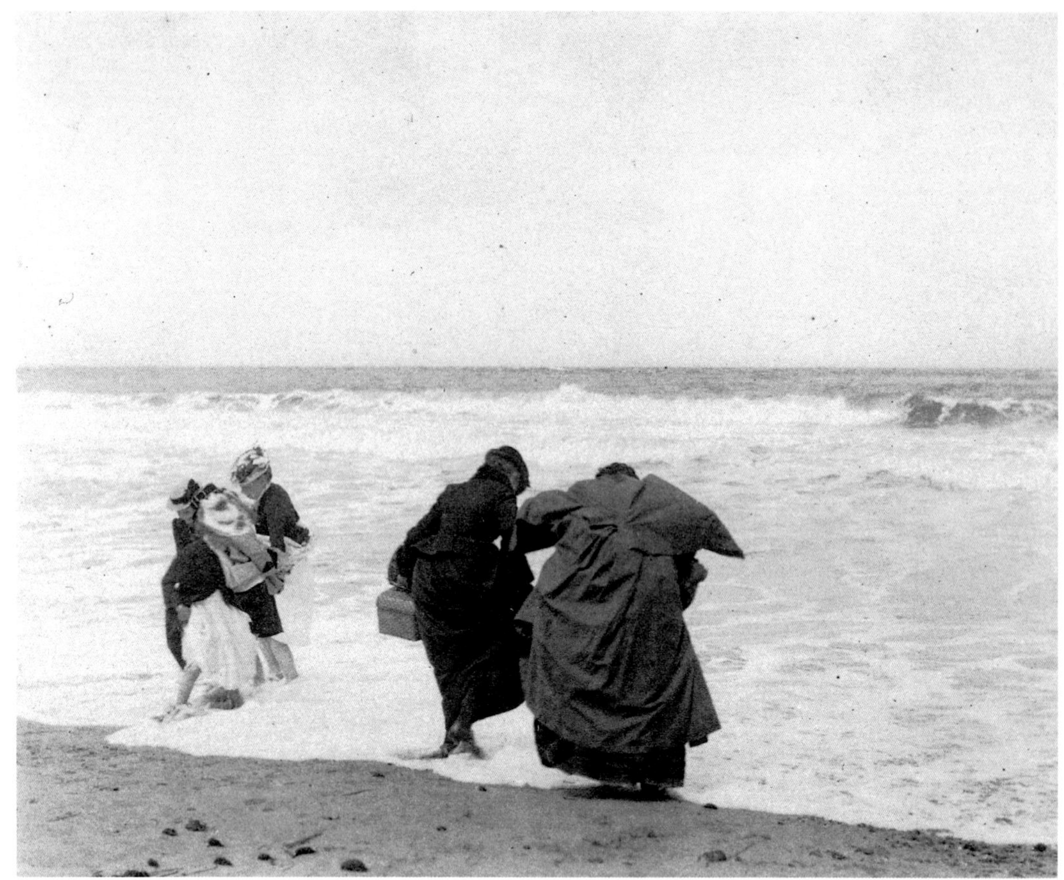

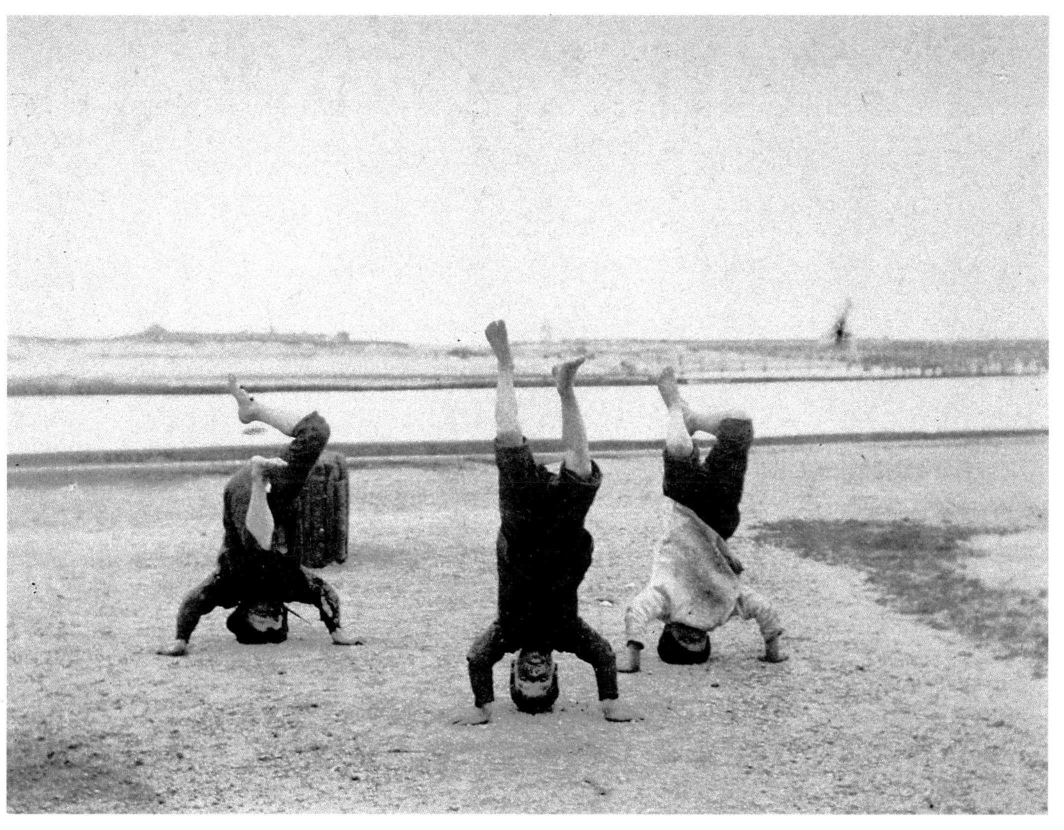

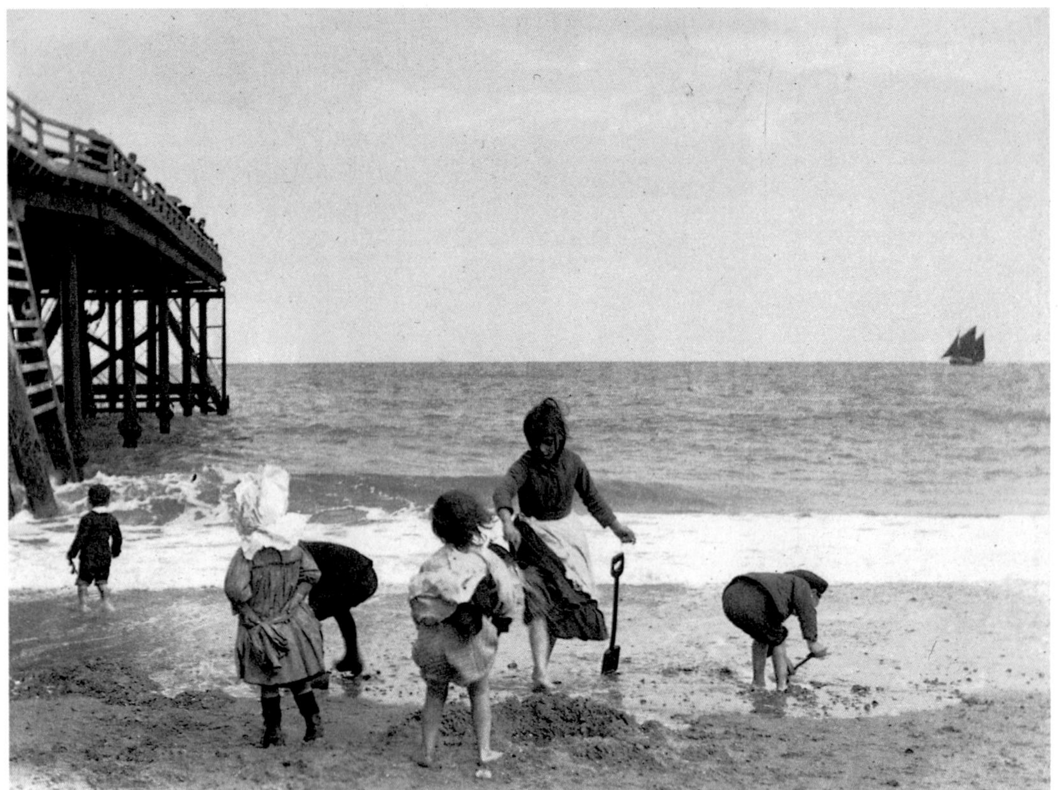

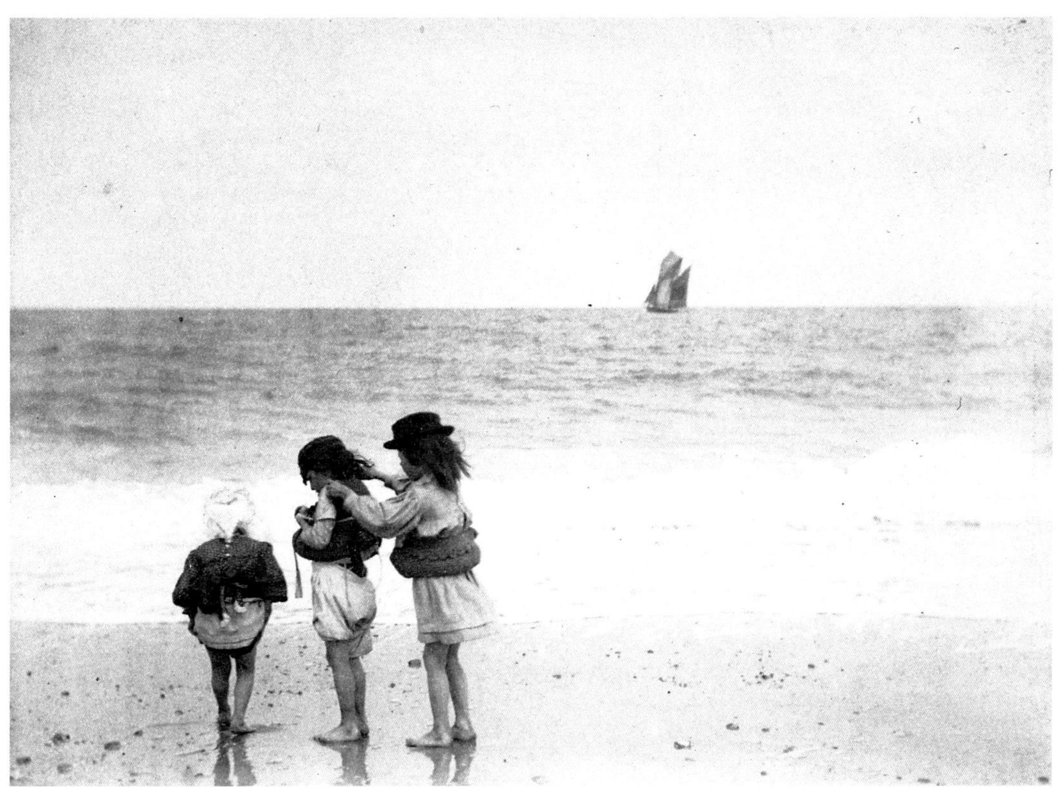

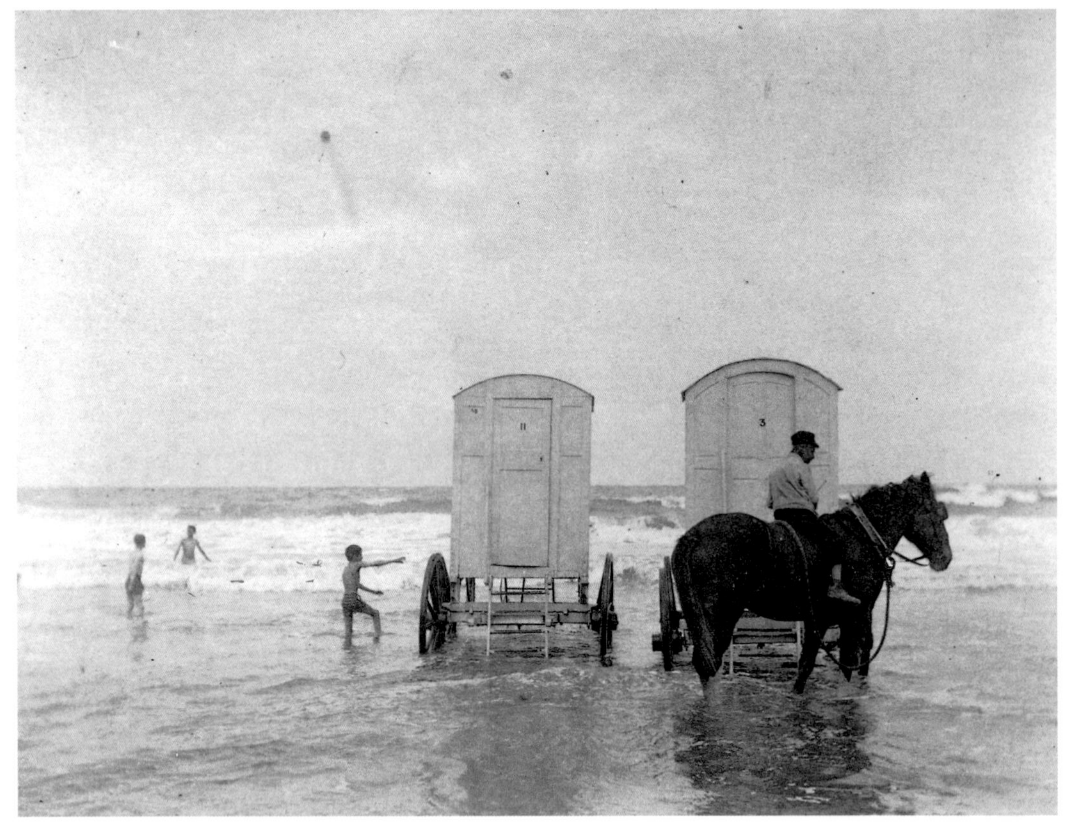

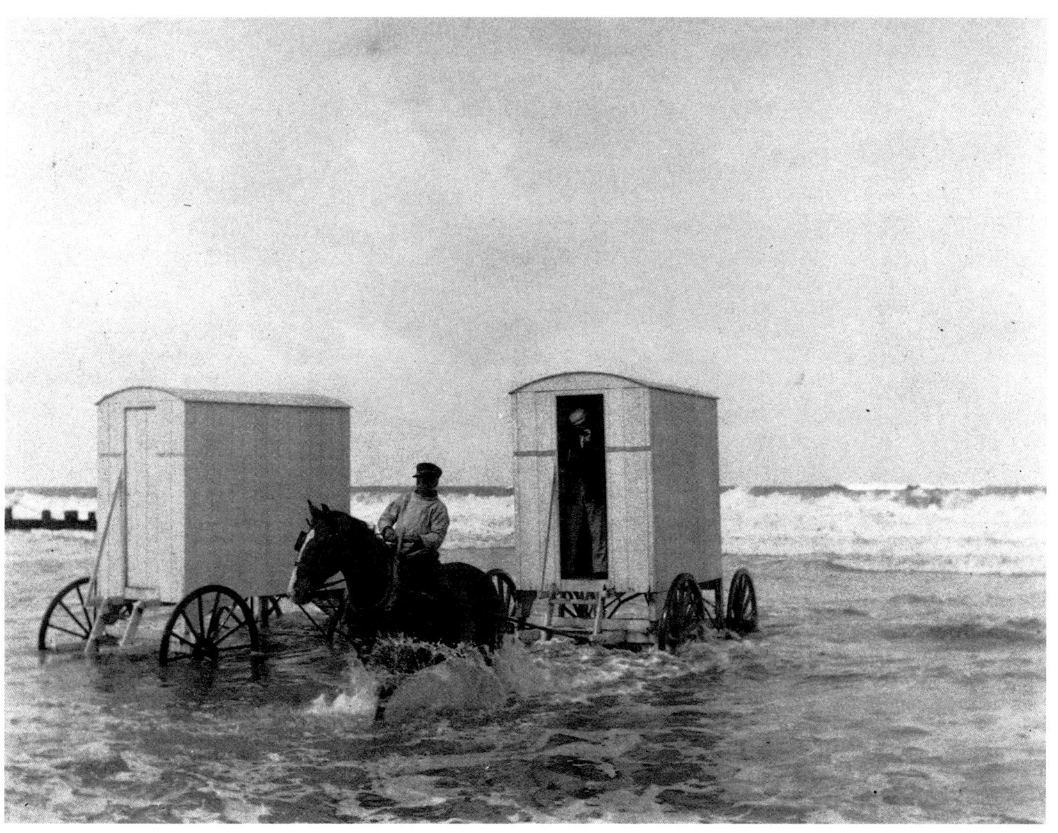

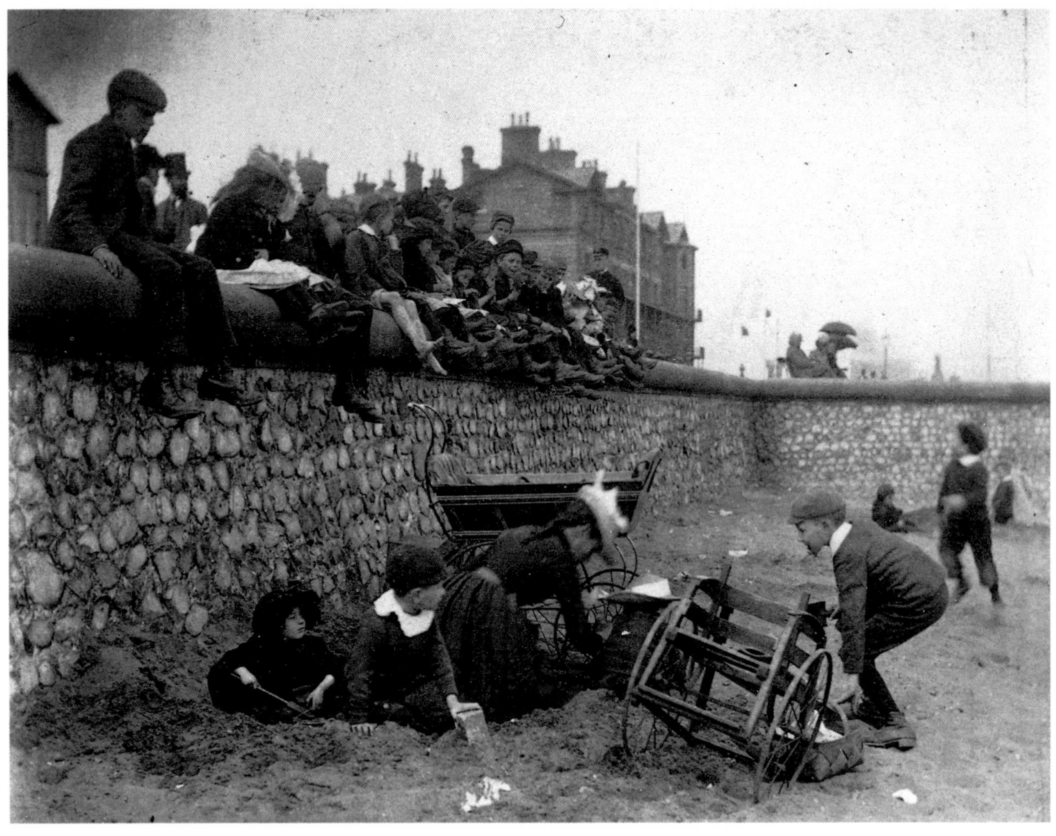

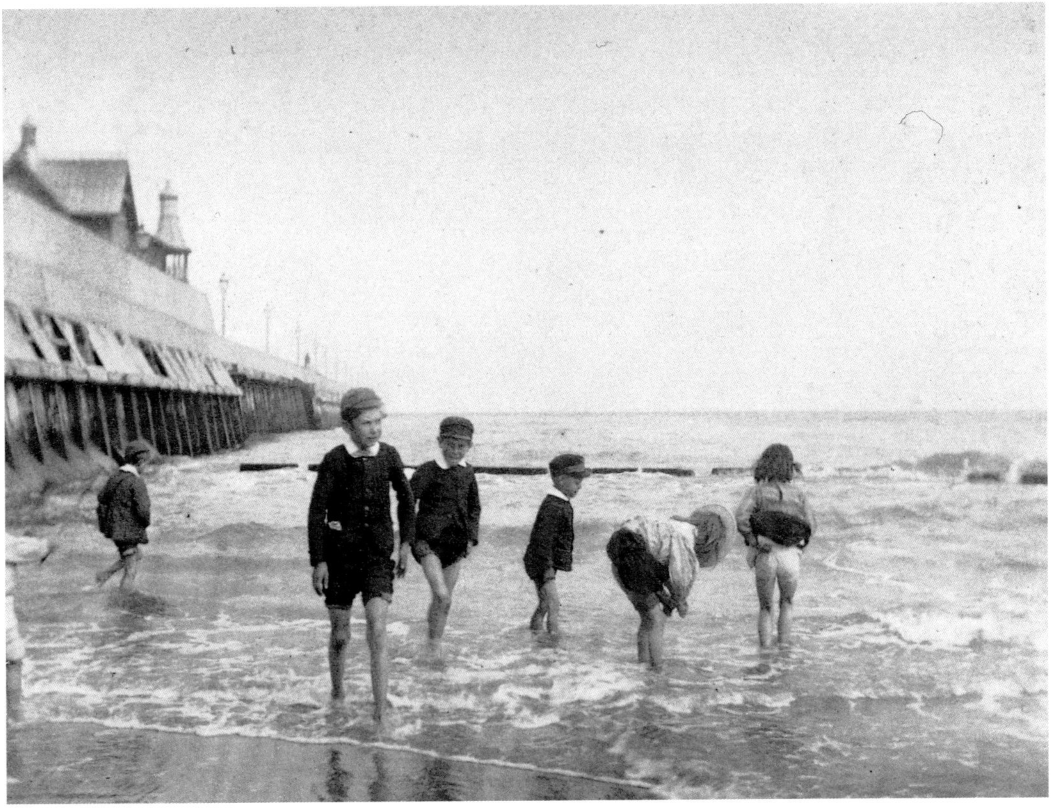

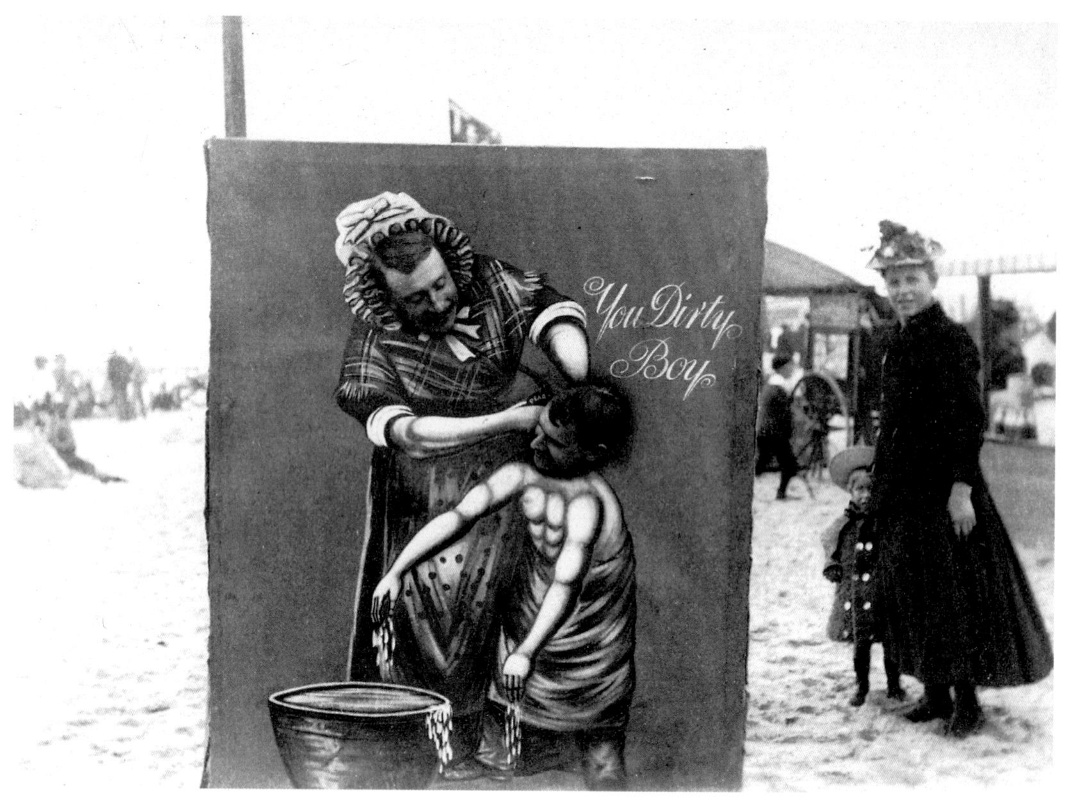
You Dirty
Boy

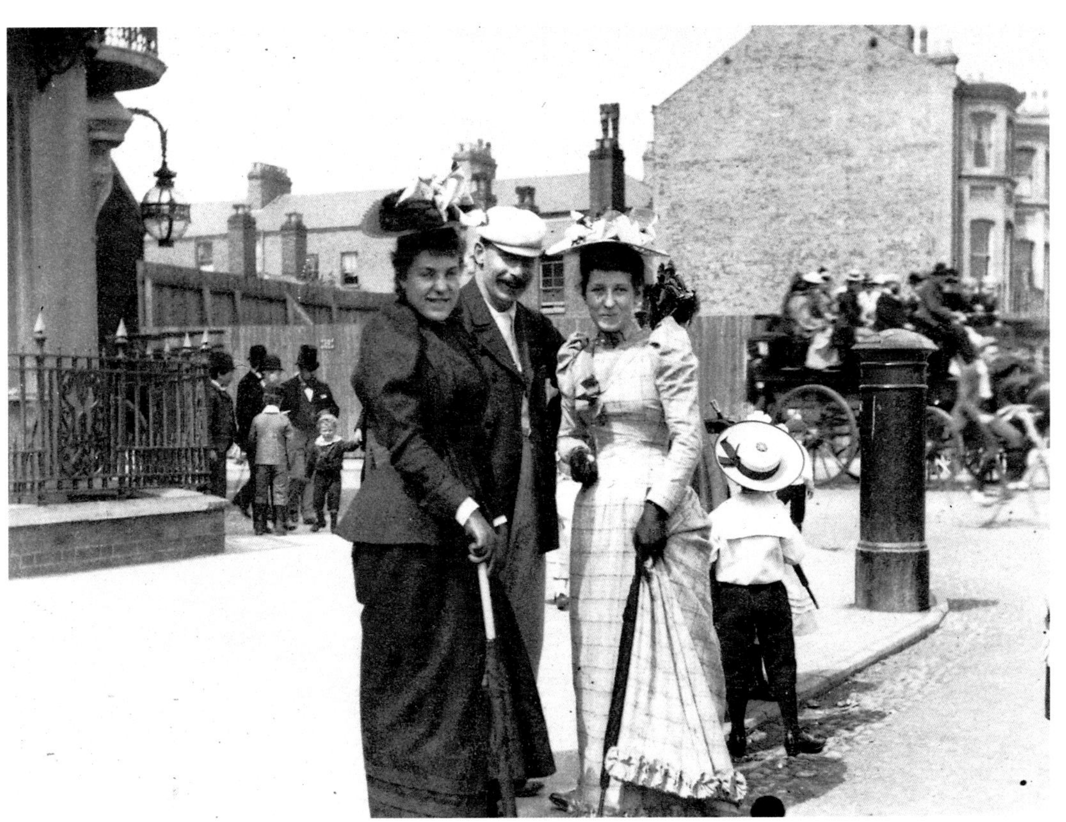

 LISTENING TO THE CONCERT PARTY ON YARMOUTH SANDS

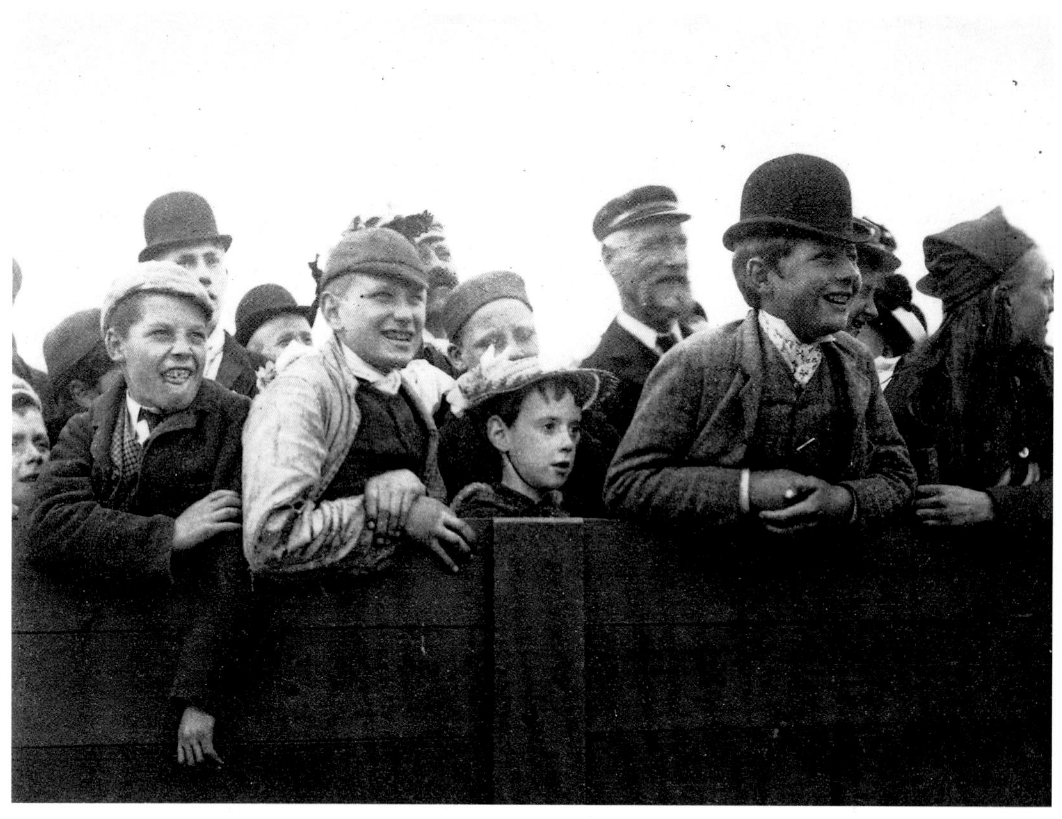

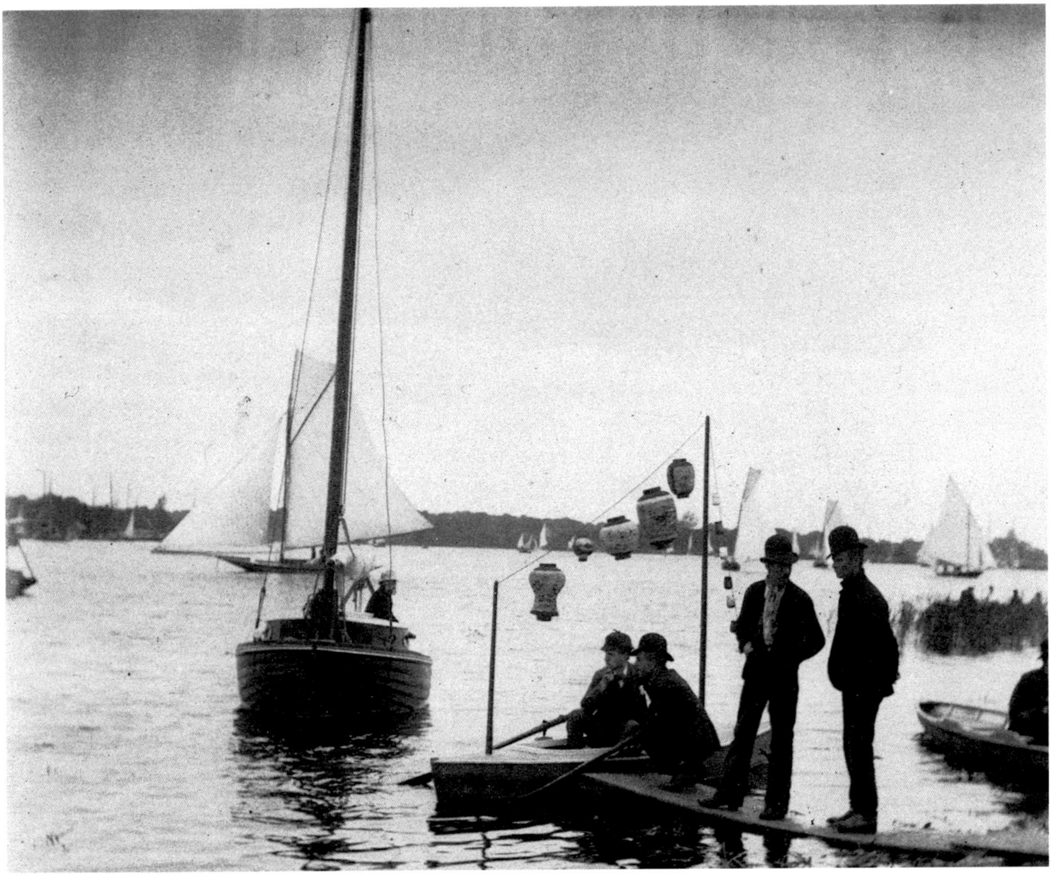

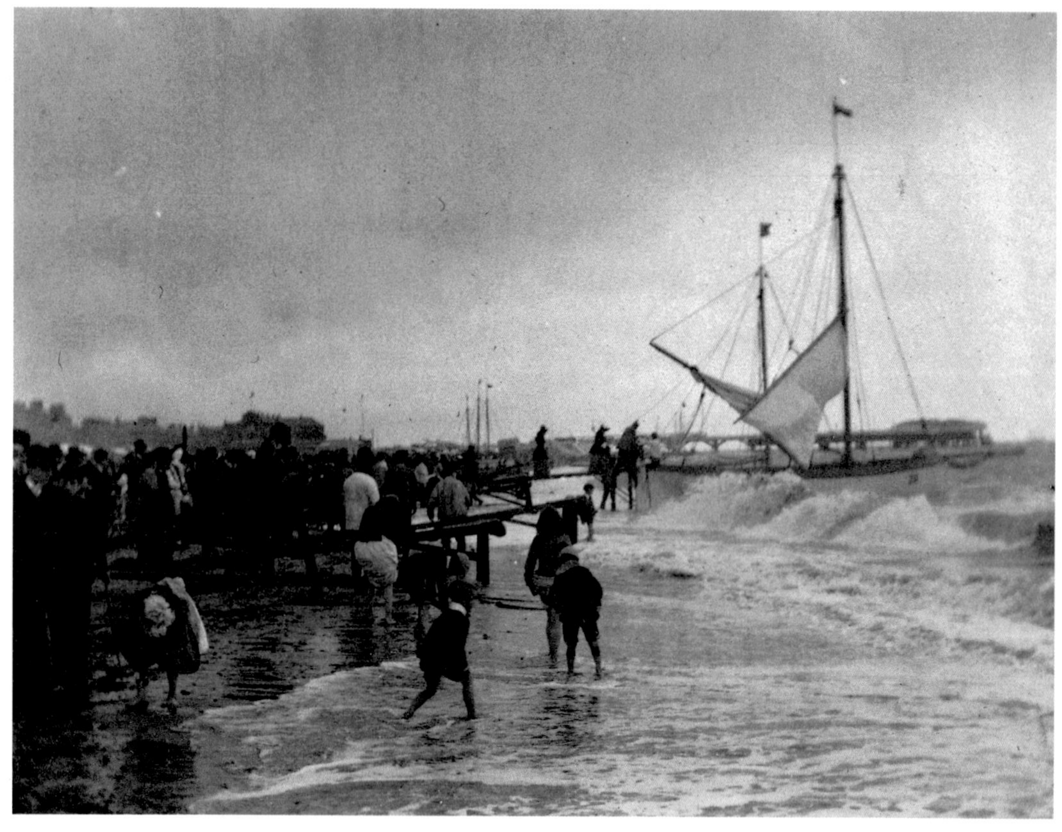

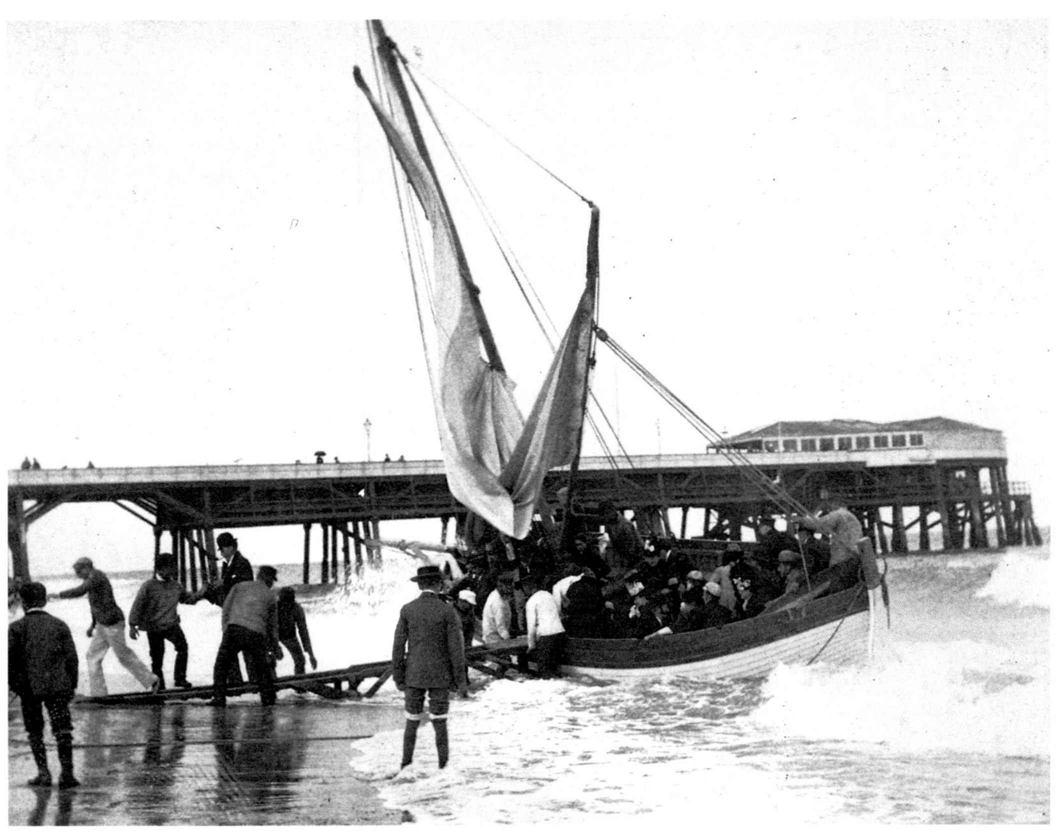

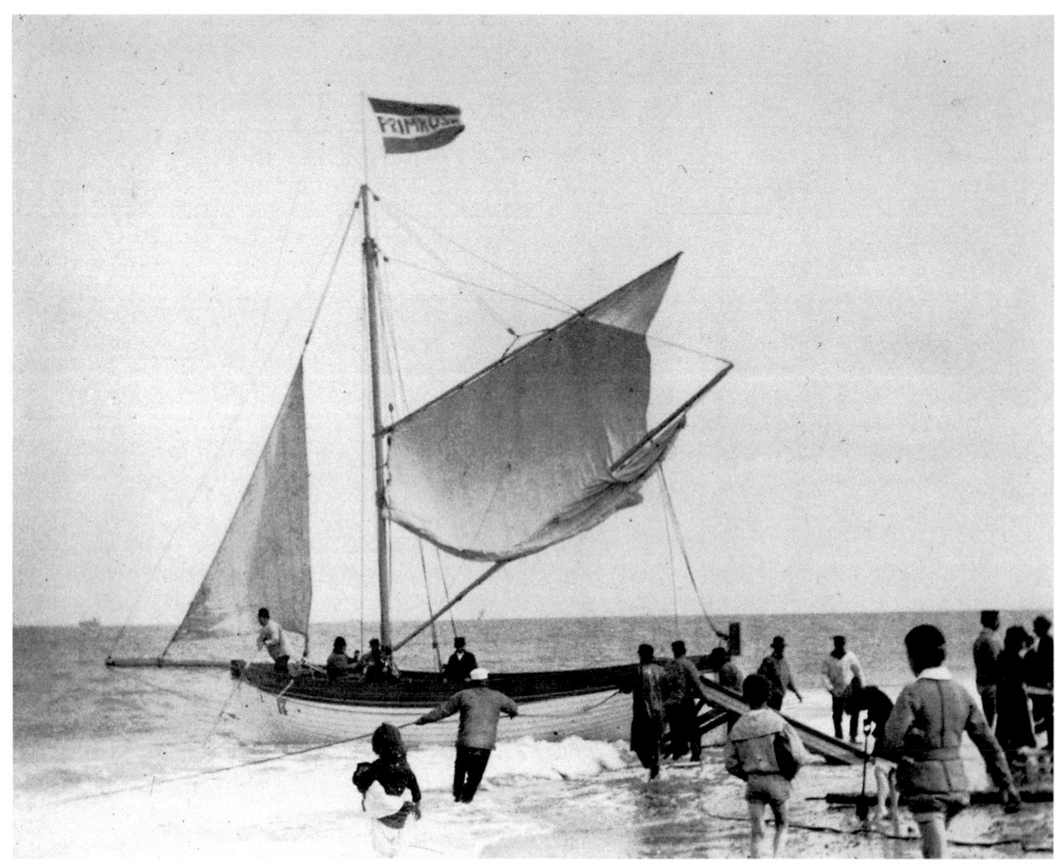

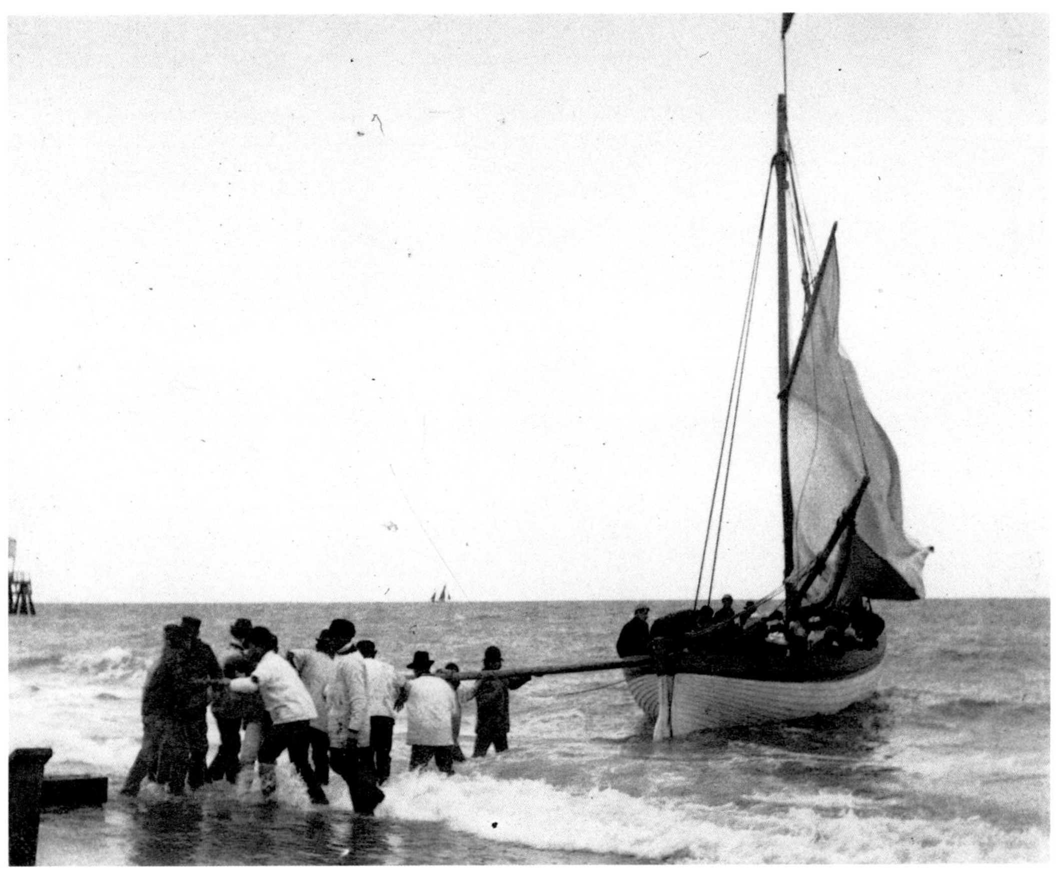

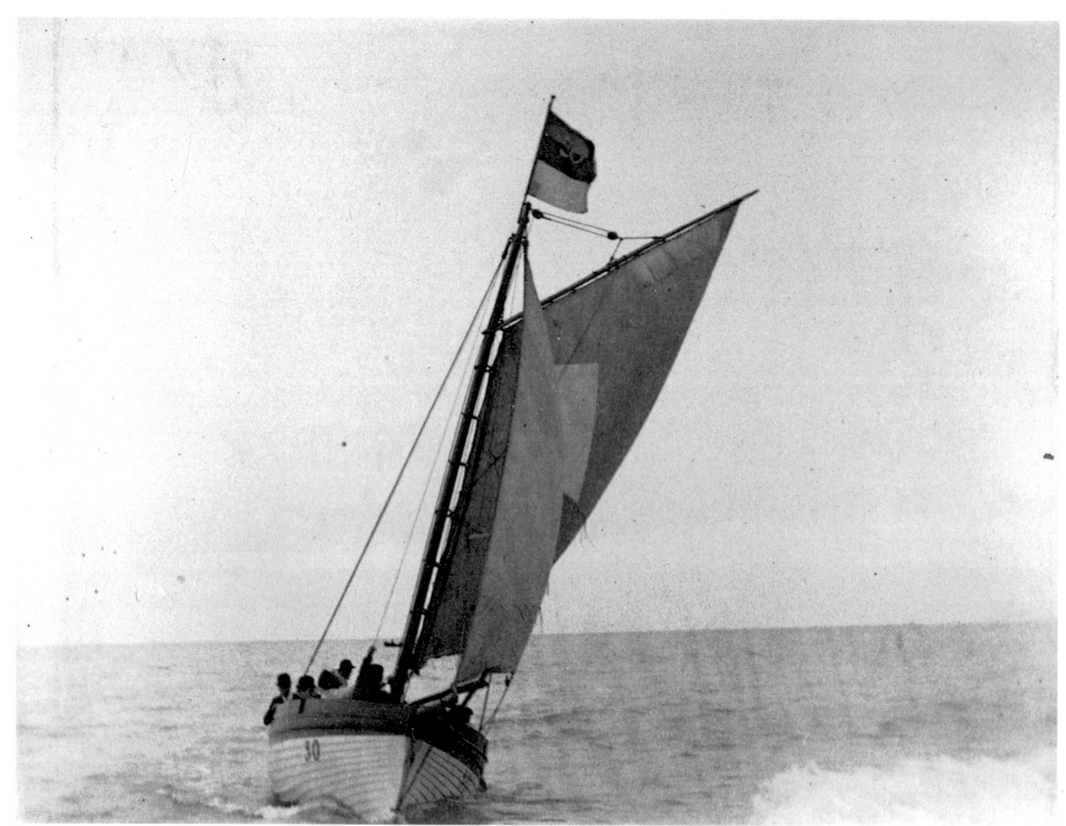
30

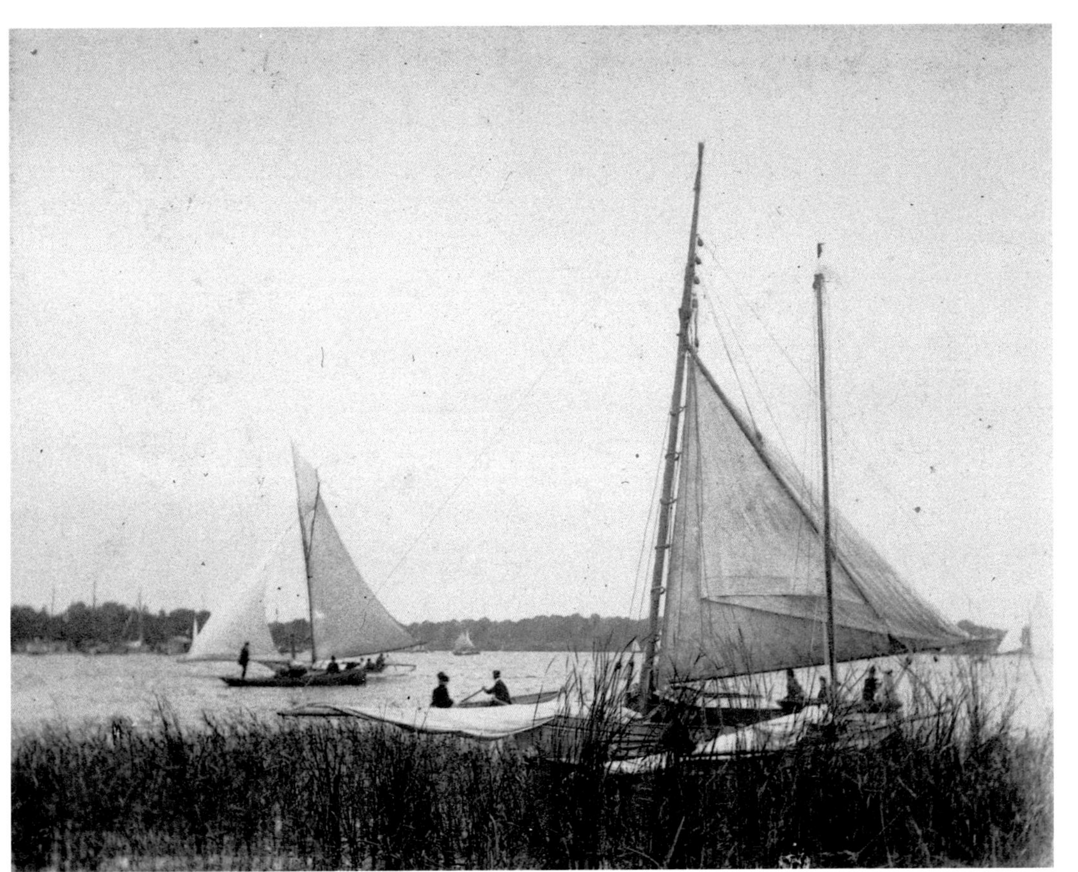

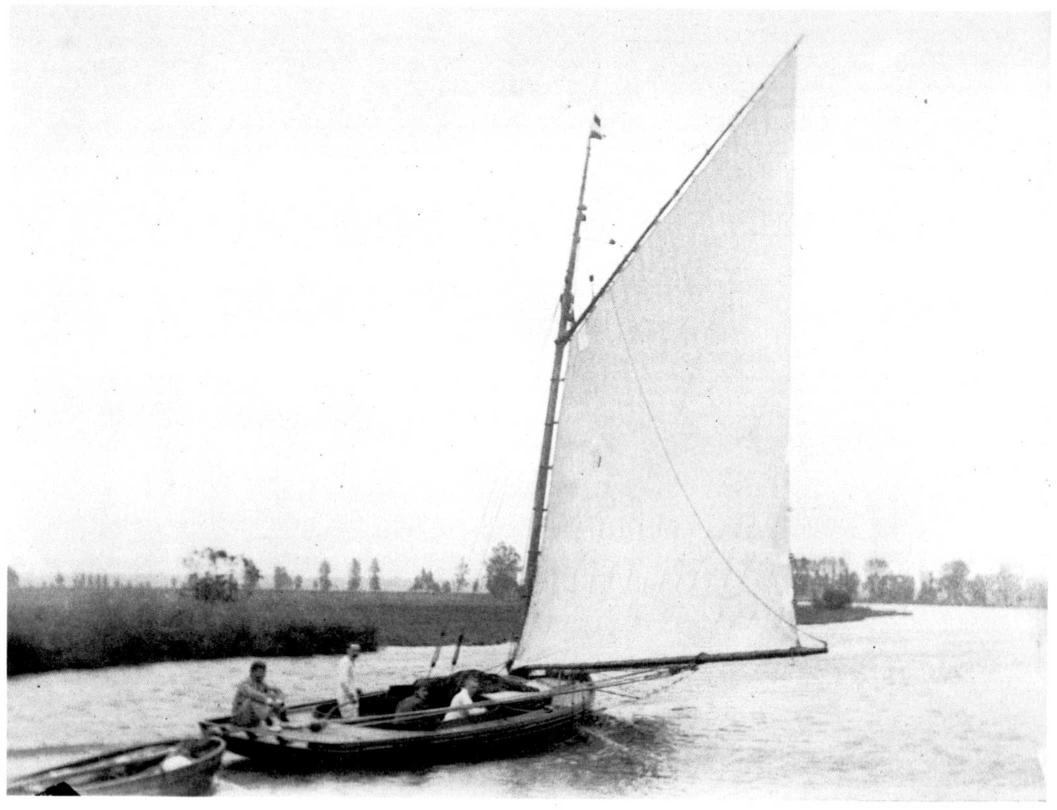

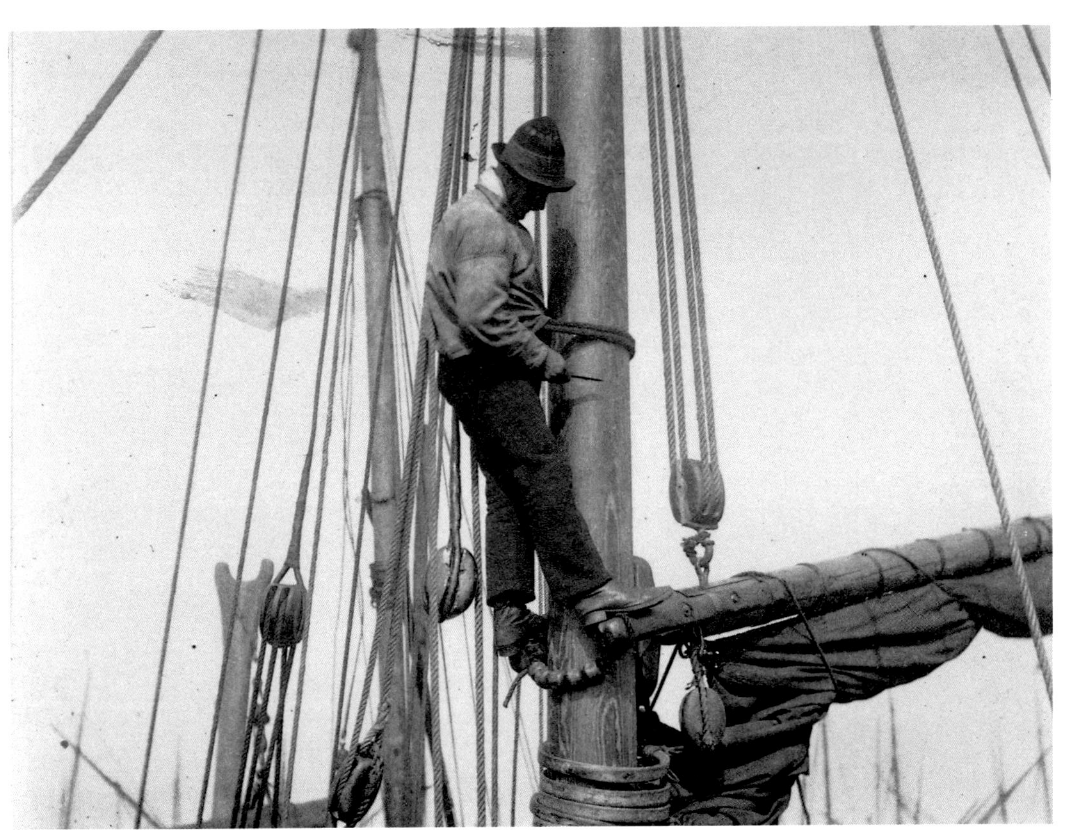

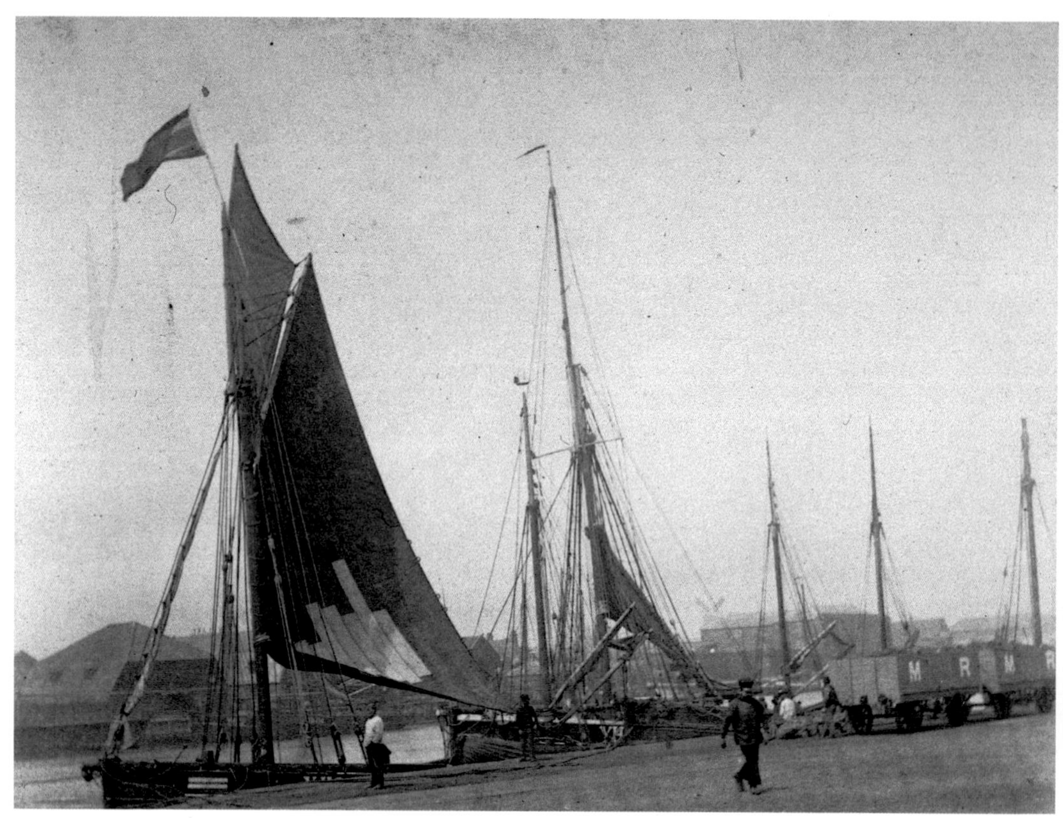
M R M R

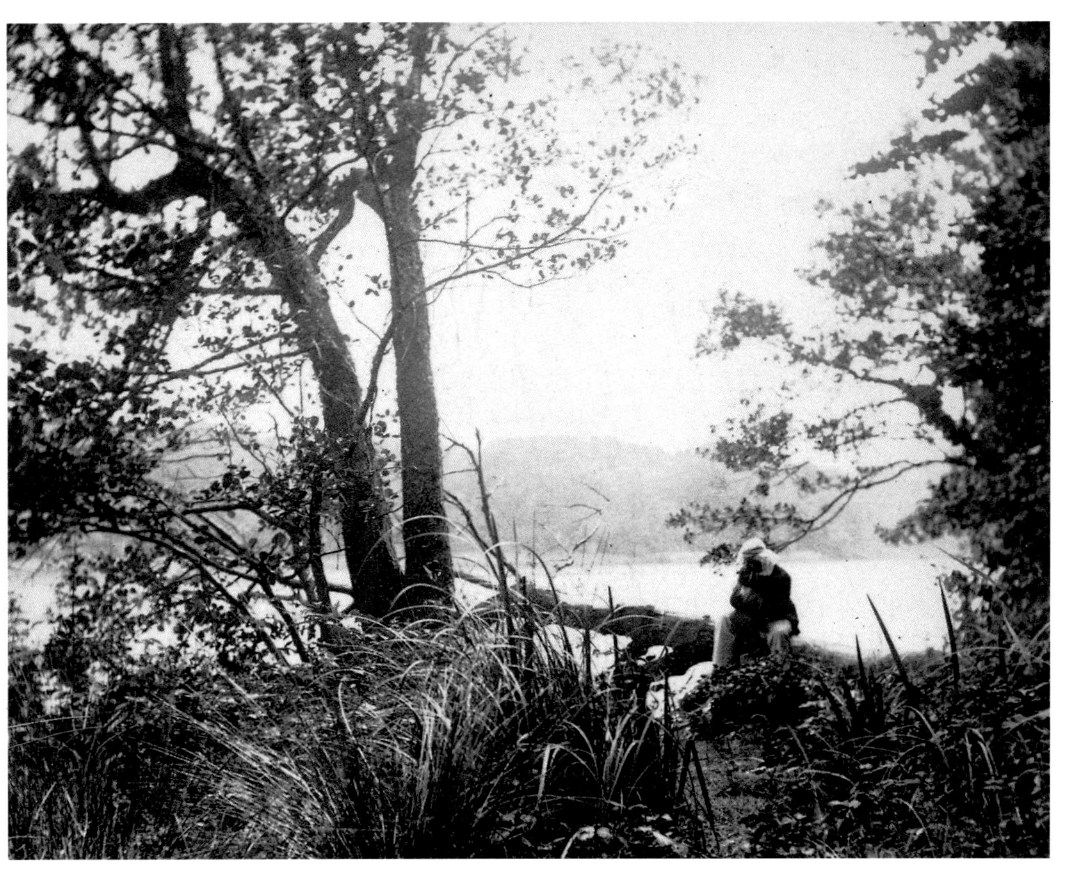

The pictures in this booklet are from the Victoria & Albert Collection. Paul Martin's photographs were printed on Platinotype, an exquisite nineteenth century paper. The album was bought by the Victoria & Albert Museum in 1978. Paul Martin's own captions are used in this booklet.

The publisher would like to thank: Mark Haworth-Booth, Curator of Photographs at the V & A; for permission to illustrate the album, The Board of Trustees, Victoria & Albert Museum; and all the other people who have assisted in the production.

Dirk Nishen will be pleased to send you further information about the Photo Library and a copy of his current catalogue

Dirk Nishen Publishing
19 Doughty Street London
WC1N 2PT Great Britain
01 242 0185

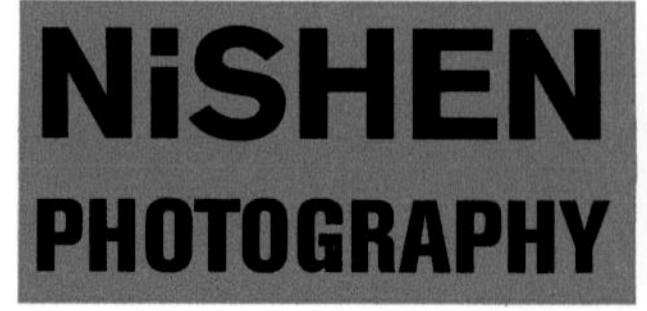

© Copyright Dirk Nishen Publishing
Text copyright Mark Haworth-Booth
Photographs copyright the Victoria & Albert Museum
All rights reserved
Set in Berthold Poppl Pontifex regular
Graphic design David Milbank Challis
Phototypesetting Nagel Phototype, D-Berlin
Origination ORT Kirchner + Graser, D-Berlin
Printing H Heenemann, D-Berlin
Binding H Hensch, D-Berlin
Printed in Germany

ISBN 1 85378 104 5